Drawings of David Cox

Alexander Joseph Finberg

Alpha Editions

This edition published in 2021

ISBN : 9789355345417

Design and Setting By
Alpha Editions
www.alphaedis.com
Email - info@alphaedis.com

As per information held with us this book is in Public Domain. This book is a reproduction of an important historical work. Alpha Editions uses the best technology to reproduce historical work in the same manner it was first published to preserve its original nature. Any marks or number seen are left intentionally to preserve its true form.

DAVID COX

THE greatest artists have expressed themselves so completely in their works, that the story of their lives adds little or nothing to our knowledge of their personality. We know very little about the life of Turner—almost as little, indeed, as we know of Shakespeare's—but in neither case do we seem to have missed anything that would add to our comprehension or enjoyment of their work. With Turner, as with Shakespeare, his art was the perfect organ of his spirit. His pictures enshrine more of the real personality of the artist than even a biographer of genius with unlimited opportunities could tell us. But though this is almost invariably true of the greatest artists, it is not true of all artists. It is hardly the case with David Cox. His hampered, thwarted art is indeed replete with glimpses and hints of the personality behind it; but without a commentary it is not very eloquent or very likely to arrest attention. The artist's life furnishes the needed commentary. The beautiful simplicity and *naïveté* of the man's character, the mean circumstances in which his life was cast, the fortitude, industry, and manliness with which he triumphed over his difficulties—these things explain much that seems at first sight futile in his art and colour even his worst failures with a glow of purely human sympathy. And the works of his old age—his most eloquent and self-subsistent productions, *i.e.*, the works of Cox that stand least in need of a commentary—these lose nothing of their compelling power from the spectator's consciousness of the difficulties through which the artist's spirit had to struggle towards self-realisation and expression.

Cox was born on April 29, 1783, in a small house, surrounded by workshops and small forges in Heath Mill Lane, Deritend, a poor suburb on the south-east side of Birmingham. His father, Joseph Cox, followed the calling of a blacksmith and whitesmith, forging gun-barrels, bayonets, horse-shoes and similar articles. He appears to have been an industrious and thriving artificer, while Cox's mother, who was better educated than his father, was a woman of forcible character, highly religious feelings and natural good sense.{8}

When about six or seven years old Cox was sent to one of the day schools in Birmingham. At this time he fell over a door-scraper and broke his leg. This accident was the cause of his first introduction to art, for a cousin gave him a box of paints to amuse himself with during the confinement which he had to endure whilst his leg was in splints. David's first artistic efforts were confined to daubing the kites which his school companions brought to him. But he was so delighted with the colours that when he recovered he procured some paper and set to work copying a number of small engravings.

After recovering from his accident he returned to school for a short time, but was soon withdrawn and set to work in his father's shop. But he was by no means a strong lad, and a short trial convinced his father that he was not fitted for so laborious a craft. With the idea of qualifying him for apprenticeship to one of the toy-trades of Birmingham, he was sent in the evenings to a drawing school in the neighbourhood, where he is said to have made great progress. At the age of fifteen David was considered capable of assisting in the ornamentation of snuff-boxes, lockets, buttons and buckles. He was apprenticed to a locket and miniature painter named Fielder. The apprenticeship, however, only lasted about a year and a half, as it was brought to an abrupt termination by the suicide of his master.

After this tragical termination of his brief experience as a locket painter and decorator Cox's cousin got him an engagement with the scene-painters employed at the Birmingham theatre. His business was to grind the colours and run errands for the painters. In the evenings he was enabled to resume his studies at his old drawing class.

The chief scene-painter at the theatre, which was leased and managed by the elder Macready, was an Italian named De Maria. Cox watched De Maria's work with great admiration, and after a time he was allowed to assist him in painting the side scenes. Upon De Maria's departure from the theatre Cox was permanently engaged with Macready as scene painter, touring with his company, and even playing small parts when occasion demanded it. At one small country place it is said that he played the part of the clown. However, the manager's hasty temper led to quarrels, and these, together with his mother's entreaties, led Cox to terminate his engagement about the year 1803.

Receiving an offer of employment from Astley, the proprietor of Astley's circus, Cox, at the age of twenty-one, moved to London. Astley's offer coming to nothing the artist had a hard time of it. {9} He executed various odd commissions for scenery for provincial theatres and disposed of small drawings at the modest rate of two guineas a dozen to various London dealers. London, however, offered more opportunities for study than Birmingham, and Cox made the most of them. He managed to become possessed of a collection of indifferent etchings from paintings by Poussin, Salvator Rosa and Claude, which had been published by Pond between 1741 and 1746. These he copied and studied for the sake of their composition and arrangement of light and shade, and a dealer named Simpson, who kept a shop in Greek Street, Soho, allowed him to make a large copy in water-colour of a fine painting by Poussin which hung in his shop. Cox's first important picture was based on the arrangement and effect of this Poussin. It is a drawing of Kenilworth Castle, an autotype of it being published in Mr. Neal Solly's admirable "Memoir of the Life of David Cox" (Chapman & Hall, 1873), a volume to which we are indebted for the details of the artist's early life. The *Kenilworth* in Mr. Solly's opinion cannot be dated later than 1806 or 1807; and to judge from the photographic reproduction it is especially interesting as an example of the imitative methods which were rife among the artists of those days. The works of the older and more successful masters were accepted as models to be copied and imitated.

In this connection it may be not impertinent to recall the account which Edward Dayes (Girtin's master) has left us of the method of education by which Turner's powers were developed. "The ways he (Turner) acquired his professional powers was by borrowing where he could a drawing or a picture to copy from, or by making a sketch of any one in the Exhibition early in the morning, and finishing it at home." So that Cox was not alone in devoting his early practice to works of art, rather than to the works of nature.

In pursuance of this plan of appropriating what he could from the practice and methods of the proficients in the art, Cox determined to take lessons from the living as well as from the dead. For some time his choice hesitated between John Varley, John Glover, and William Havell. He finally decided to go to Varley, who treated him with much kindness. Varley, who was only five years older than Cox, was one of the most successful teachers of the time, and, in addition to Cox, he numbered Mulready, W. H. Hunt, Linnell, Samuel Palmer, Copley Fielding, and De Windt among his pupils. His early manner was modelled largely on the practice of John Cozens and Girtin; and the simplicity, directness and dignity of much of Cox's early work is certainly due to the thoroughness{10} with which Varley had mastered the traditions of the earlier English water-colour painters, and to his capacities as a teacher. The second plate in this volume is a reproduction of one of Cox's drawings of this period. The original water-colour, *Old Westminster*, is probably one of the most successful of Cox's purely architectural drawings; it might almost pass for a Girtin.

In 1805, Cox made his first journey into Wales. He supported himself at this time by working up the sketches made on such tours, and by chance commissions for scenery. A bill is still in existence, dated February 15, 1808, for "painting 310 yards of scenery at 4s. per square yard." The year when he executed this lucrative commission was the year of his marriage to the eldest daughter of the landlady in whose house at Lambeth Cox had lodged since his arrival in London. His wife, who was eight years his senior, is said to have been a slight, delicate woman, of a naturally cheerful disposition. The young couple rented a small cottage at the corner of Dulwich Common, "just past the College on the road to the right." Dulwich Common at that time was a wild and lonely spot, much frequented by gypsies, whose donkeys and picturesque rags and surroundings formed excellent material for the young artist's compositions.

To eke out his meagre resources, Cox now turned his attention to teaching. He was fortunate enough to attract the attention of Colonel the Hon. H. Windsor (afterwards Earl of Plymouth), who took many lessons from him, and introduced and recommended him to several families of distinction. But the times were bad for artists, and the newly married couple must have found it hard work to make both ends meet. From some extracts from the artist's account book, which Mr. Solly has printed, we learn that Cox's prices for lessons ranged from 7*s*. to 10*s*. Between 1811 and 1814 the prices he got for his drawings ranged from half-a-guinea up to five guineas. His average price seems to have been about a guinea a drawing; but on November 30, 1811, he sold a dozen for 8*s*. each.

Nearly every year during his residence in London, Cox made a journey to visit his old father and his other friends at Birmingham. The sketch book he used on his 1810 visit is still in existence, and Plate XVIII., a drawing of some half-timbered houses "near Birmingham," represents the contents of one of its pages. The drawings are all made on rough blue paper; and among the other subjects contained in this singularly interesting book are some striking studies of scenes down a mine at Dudley, and sketches at and near Kenilworth. The handling is not so loose as in Cox's later work;{11} but what the drawings lack in freedom is more than compensated by their directness and admirable restraint, as our reproduction amply proves.

During the period of the artist's early married life he had many difficulties to contend with. The long war with France had depressed trade, made living dear, and people generally had little to spare for articles of luxury. But Cox worked away steadily at his art, forming himself on the best models. This was the time when Turner was painting what many artists consider are among the finest landscapes that have ever been produced by an English artist. His *Sun rising through Vapour*, the picture which now hangs in the National Gallery beside the Claudes, was exhibited in 1807, the *Spithead* in 1809, and the superb *Windsor*, *Abingdon*, *Greenwich*, and *Frosty Morning*, were all painted and exhibited within the next few years. The first number of the "Liber," too, appeared in 1807; and as one turns over the plates that were issued in the earlier numbers—designs like the *Flint Castle*, *Barn and Straw Yard*, *Pembury Mill*, *Morpeth*, and *Lock and Mill*—it is easy to imagine the influence they must have exerted on the formation of Cox's art. We have it on Mr. Solly's authority that "no artist appreciated Turner's genius more than Cox did," and he illustrates this with a charming anecdote of Cox's reproduction from memory of Turner's picture of *Kingston Bank* (now in the National Gallery). Mr. Solly also states that Cox was one of the earliest subscribers to the "Liber," and he adds, "that he did so at this time, when his means were so straitened, is a proof how highly he prized this admirable work." The remark is perfectly just, though it may be worth remembering that those were the times when ordinary issues of the "Liber" were still to be had for a modest 15*s.* for a part containing five plates.

With such models before his eyes it is not surprising to find that Cox's work at this period is characterised by a breadth of style, a feeling of repose, and an absence of any attempt at superficial prettiness or drawing-master dexterity. But though Cox became a member of the Society of Painters in Water-Colour in 1813, and contributed no less than seventeen drawings to its Exhibition, few of them found purchasers. In the summer of this year Cox was glad to accept an appointment as teacher of drawing at the Military College at Farnham. But the work and military discipline to which he had to submit proved irksome, and at the end of a term or two he was allowed to retire. Soon after this, in 1814, Cox went to Hereford, having accepted a post as drawing-master at a young ladies' school. This new appointment carried with it the magnificent salary {12} of £100 a year, but he had to teach only twice a week, and he was at liberty to take private pupils.

The removal to Hereford, where the artist remained for thirteen years, is rightly regarded by Cox's biographers as an important event in his life. He went there penniless, having indeed to borrow £40 to defray the expenses of his removal, and he left there with at least a thousand pounds to the good. The money, it is true, was amassed slowly and with difficulty, and it was earned rather by incessant teaching than by original artistic productivity. But the town was pleasantly situated; the Wye winds round the city walls, and Wales is not far distant. Cox had opportunities for familiarising himself with all the details of rustic business—with ploughing, haymaking, reaping, and sowing; and in his constant journeyings to and fro for the purpose of giving lessons his memory became stored with images of all kinds of weather and all kinds of effects.

All the coloured reproductions in the present volume represent drawings made during the artist's residence in Hereford. The *Chepstow Bridge and Castle* (Plate XII.) was probably one of the results of Cox's first sketching tour after his removal, and this very drawing may possibly have formed one of the exhibits which he sent to the Society of Painters in Water-Colour in 1816. Plate XXIII. may represent the sketch made for the picture of *Goodrich Castle on the Wye*, which the artist exhibited in 1819. In both the drawings, as in the unfinished Frontispiece, the colour scheme is less severe than in the earlier *Westminster*. They are less like Girtin's than like early Cotmans; and though they lack something of Cotman's fastidiousness of selection, and the aristocratic charm of his draughtsmanship and design, they have a sobriety, reserve and seriousness of their own which must make them objects of delight to their fortunate possessor. The slightness of the execution of *Low Tide* (Plate XXXIV.) is no hindrance to the poignant expression of its sentiment. Unfortunately, it has not been found convenient to reproduce the magnificent—albeit unfinished—water-colour, entitled *Autumn Woods*, in its original colours. The half-tone reproduction (Plate XIX.), however, is useful as a suggestion of the simple dignity that reigns in this beautiful drawing—assuredly one of the finest works produced during the artist's residence in Hereford.

It is interesting to learn that the production in great quantities of small drawings like those we have reproduced in colour, and his onerous duties of teaching, did not exhaust Cox's energies. At that time Cox was something of a politician. Very naturally he took great delight in the raciness and full-flavoured eloquence of Cobbet{13}t's "Register"; and in 1820, when Joseph Hume visited Hereford, Cox, as one of the advanced Liberals of the locality, formed one of the committee of reception, and with two others subscribed to present the reformer with a hogshead of the best Herefordshire cider. A public dinner was organised at which to make the presentation, and on his return home in the evening Cox decided to celebrate so important a day by planting a number of acorns and chestnuts in his garden. But Cox's reforming zeal was not always satisfied with such unaggressive results. As a protest against the policy of the Government which led to the imposition of high taxes on tea, beer and other articles of domestic consumption, he determined to slake his thirst with non-dutiable beverages. He religiously drank Hunt's roasted corn for a time, but finding the concoction unpalatable he invented a beverage of his own. He and his unfortunate family drank a concoction made from new hay in place of tea-leaves as a morning beverage; but, in the long run, the iniquitous revenue triumphed.

Even now, however, we have not come to the end of Cox's multifarious activities during this period. Besides being an amateur agitator and gardener, a prolific artist in water colour, and an overworked teacher, he seems to have turned author as well. In 1814 he published an educational work on landscape art, called: "A Treatise on Landscape Painting and Effect in Water-Colours, from the first Rudiments to the finished Picture, with Examples in Outline Effect and Colouring." This was illustrated by a number of soft-ground etchings. It was followed, in 1816, by "Progressive Lessons in Landscape for Young Beginners," a series of twenty-four soft-ground etchings without letterpress; and in 1825, his

"Young Artist's Companion, or Drawing-Book of Studies," appeared. It was perhaps as a preliminary study for one of the illustrations to these volumes that the pen and ink drawing reproduced in Plate XIV. was made. At any rate the interest of these publications depends rather upon the illustrations than upon the letterpress, many of the etchings containing the first ideas of subjects which later had great success as water-colours; the etchings of *Changing Pasture* and *Going to the Mill*, for example, furnished the subjects of some of Cox's latest paintings. It has also been rumoured that Cox was not entirely responsible for the letterpress, being indebted for assistance in its composition to some unknown "clergyman." However this may be, it is pretty certain that the opinions must have been those which Cox himself held. And as the opinions of a great artist as to the aim and scope of his own art are always of interest it may be {14} advisable to quote a passage or two from these books, even though some other hand may have corrected the artist's grammar and inflated his periods.

In the "Treatise" Cox writes: "The principal art of Landscape Painting consists in conveying to the mind the most forcible effect which can be produced from the various classes of scenery.... This is the grand principle upon which pictorial excellence hinges, as many pleasing objects, the combination of which renders a piece perfect, are frequently passed over by an observer because the whole of the composition is not under the influence of a suitable effect. Thus a cottage or a village scene requires a soft and simple admixture of tones calculated to produce pleasure without astonishment. On the contrary, the structures of greatness and antiquity should be marked by a character of awful sublimity, suited to the dignity of the subjects, indenting on the mind a reverential and permanent impression, and giving at once a corresponding and unequivocal grandeur to the picture. Much depends on the classification of the objects, which should wear a magnificent uniformity, and much on the colouring, the tones of which should be deep and impressive.

"In the selection of a subject from nature the student should ever keep in view the principal object which induced him to make the sketch, whether it be mountains, a castle, group of trees, a cornfield, river scene, or any other object. The prominence of this leading feature in the piece should be duly supported throughout; the character of the picture should be derived from it; every other object introduced should be subservient to it, and the attraction of the one should be the attraction of the whole. The union of too great a variety of parts tends to destroy, or at least to weaken, the predominance of that which ought to be the principal of the composition, and which the student, when he comes to the colouring, should be careful to characterise by turning upon it the strongest light. All objects which are not in character with the scenes should be most carefully avoided, as the introduction of any unnecessary object is sure to be attended with injurious consequences. This must prove the necessity of becoming thoroughly acquainted with and obtaining a proper feeling of the subject. The picture should be complete and perfect in the mind before it is ever traced upon canvas. Such force and expression should be displayed as would render the effect at the first glance intelligible to the observer. Merely to paint is not enough, for when no interest is felt nothing is more natural than that none should be conveyed."

And again: "The last and surest method of obtaining instruction {15} from the works of others is not so much by copying them as by drawing the same subjects from nature immediately after a critical examination of them, while they are fresh in the memory. Thus they are seen through the same medium, and imitated upon the same principles, without preventing the introduction of sufficient alterations to give originality of manner, or incurring the risk of being degraded into a mere imitator."

In the frequent wordiness and emptiness of parts of these passages it is easy to trace the hand of the friendly clergyman. But through it all one can catch the echoes of Cox's own convictions. He has realised very clearly the need that the colour and light and shade of a drawing should be emotionally expressive as well as merely explanatory. Cox was no realist in the shallow sense of the term; he was as convinced an idealist as Reynolds himself, and as firmly opposed to the scientific and abstract conception of art as a merely optical exercise divorced from the primary feelings and emotions of humanity.

After thirteen years' residence in Hereford, Cox determined to return to London. He felt the need for opportunities of intercourse with his brother artists and for a wider scope for his art. When he had left London at the end of 1814 he had been surrounded by difficulties, and his prospects had seemed far from bright. But in 1827 the outlook had brightened. The trade of the country, fostered by many years of peace, was now flourishing, and Cox himself was now possessed of a certain but very small income. For though Cox's name was by this time fairly well known in the world of art he had often to face the unpleasant experience of finding the whole of the twenty or thirty drawings he had exhibited with the Water Colour Society returned unsold. When his drawings did sell they commanded only very small prices, as the following entry from his account book shows:

"1830.

> July 5. Five water-colour drawings, *viz.*, *Calais Pier*, *View in Ghent*, *Boat in the Scheldt near Dort*, *Minehead*, and *Landscape in Wales*—price for the five, £12."

It was not till about 1836 that anything like a sustained demand for his work came into existence. Even then, it was only his smaller drawings that he could readily dispose of, and these only at the modest prices of £5 or £6 each. Consequently, in London as in Hereford, it was upon his work as a drawing-master that Cox had to rely for the main part of his income.

It can scarcely be doubted that the effect upon Cox's art of this {16} constant drudgery of teaching was mischievous. Besides frittering away the best part of his time, thus preventing him from attempting works that required sustained efforts, it had a tendency to force a mechanical and facile dexterity upon his style—a quality hopelessly at variance with all the most sincerely felt contents of his work. For the business of the drawing-master in those days was very different from that which now devolves upon an art-master. To-day a teacher of art does little more than criticise the work which his pupils produce. In Cox's time a drawing-master had to go from one pupil's house to another, making a display of his own accomplishments. His lessons resolved themselves into the making of show pieces. He sat down before the pupil and "showed how it was done," and the professional success of the teacher depended largely upon the admiration he could excite in his pupils or their parents and guardians at the apparent ease and rapidity with which he could manufacture plausible imitations of works of art. That the habit of working to excite the astonishment of the ignorant and uncritical tended to bring something of commonness into Cox's style can hardly be doubted. That the daily round of making a show of himself and his beloved art must have been peculiarly galling to a man of Cox's simple and transparently honest nature, needs little evidence. We can scarcely wonder when his sympathetic biographer tells us that at times he would say to his wife, "Oh, Mary, I cannot go out this morning to teach—I feel I cannot do it." At these times it required all his wife's powers of persuasion to induce him to overcome his repugnance; often she had to put on her bonnet and mantle and accompany him to the pupil's house.

In 1840, *i.e.*, at the age of fifty-seven, Cox determined to cut himself free from these depressing duties, and to devote the remainder of his days to more purely artistic labours. By his own and his wife's frugality he had been able to save enough money to secure his old age against want, and his son, who was now married and settled in London as an artist, was able and willing to take over his father's teaching connection. Besides, Cox was tired of the noise and bustle of London, and anxious to live among more rural surroundings. He therefore began to look out for a house on the outskirts of Birmingham, his native town. His choice fell upon an old house in Greenfield Lane, in the village of Harborne, about two and a half miles from Birmingham, into which he and his wife moved on June 20, 1841.

The house stood in a lane leading to Harborne Church, beyond which meadows and open country stretched out in the direction of{17} Hagley. The garden was a large one, surrounded on both sides by trees, and Cox took great interest in it, often working there himself. He enjoyed cultivating broad-leaved plants, such as rhubarb and the various kinds of docks, and he was especially fond of Scotch thistles and hollyhocks. At Harborne, he spent some of the happiest years of his life; he was happy in his home, in his work, and in his surroundings. As Mr. Solly says, "Cox's wants were few and simple; his ambition took no flight beyond the constant aim of his life, namely, to excel in the practice of his art. The inexhaustible wealth of nature, his genius, and the love of his family and friends, sufficed to fill his cup with more happiness than is allotted to most men; even when his steps were fast approaching that goal to which all human efforts tend, he was still serene and generally cheerful." We need not wonder that the most moving and powerful of all the artist's works were painted after his removal to Harborne.

From 1841 to the end in 1859, Cox's artistic career was one of unbroken, though limited, success. The weight of years only strengthened the grim certainty with which he grasped the essentials of his art. All his drawing-master dexterity gradually fell away from him, the trivialities of imitative and explanatory art were quietly eliminated, and his art took on the simplicity, the sincerity, and rugged human dignity of the man's own character.

Of the visits to Bettwys-y-Coed, of the painting of such masterpieces as *The Welsh Funeral, The Peat Gatherers, Lancaster Sands, Green Lanes,* and *Going to the Hayfield,* of his superb work in oil colour, and indeed of all the closing events of the artist's life, it is impossible here to speak in detail. The whole story has been well and fully told by admiring friends like Mr. Hall and Mr. Solly, who were intimately associated with the life they describe, and to whose pages the reader may be warmly recommended.

Reproductions of a number of charcoal and chalk sketches belonging to this later period of his life have been included in the present volume. Large charcoal drawings like *The Salt Marsh* (Plate XXV.), *The Beach* (Plate XXVII.), *Windy Weather* (Plate XXVIII.), and *The Hill Side* (Plate XXXIII.), lose something of their impressiveness when reduced in size, as these have necessarily been, but enough remains, even in this form, of their freshness, largeness of conception and sense of movement, to delight the intelligent amateur. No one at all susceptible to the higher beauties of art could remain insensible to the fascination of the bold, synthetic handling of *The Peasants on Horseback* (Plate III.). In some of these late sketches—notably in the two *Near Kenilworth* (Plates VII.{18} and XXIV.)—the loose, flowing touch often seems a trifle too disdainful of the individual forms of objects. But when the artist is serenely self-possessed his style is delightfully intimate and unbuttoned, a candid revelation of his sympathies and moods. When thoroughly interested he becomes astonishingly vivid and succinct, as in the *Kirkby Stephen* (Plate XX.), *Llanrwst* (Plate XVI.), and *Clapham, Yorkshire* (Plate XXII.). How much his art had become a matter of feeling and impulse is shown by the glaring way he fails when his sympathies have not been aroused; the draughtsmanship of the *Architectural Study* (Plate XXII.) is about as bad as draughtsmanship can well be—bald, perfunctory, external. The pencil and stump drawing of *Carnarvon Castle* (Plate XXX.), for all its lightness and charm of atmospheric suggestion, is "mappy" in draughtsmanship—its drawing being mere "spacing," without intimacy in the form or sympathy with the structure. The drawing of *Rotterdam* (Plate XLI.) is again external and unsympathetic. These drawings might well have been chosen as illustrations of the truth of one of Cox's own remarks: "Merely to paint" (or draw) "is not enough, for when no interest is felt nothing is more natural than that none should be conveyed."

From the passages quoted above from his "Treatise on Landscape Painting and Effect"—in which this remark occurs—it is evident that Cox must be classed among the Idealists rather than among the Realists or Naturalists. The character of a picture, he insists, should be determined by the character and appropriate sentiments of its principal object; "every other object introduced should be subservient to it, and the attraction of the one should be the attraction of the whole," he writes. He insists upon the necessity "of becoming thoroughly acquainted with and obtaining a proper feeling of the subject," and maintains that "the picture should be complete and perfect in the mind before it is ever traced upon the canvas." And these were undoubtedly the principles upon which his finest works were wrought. It is obviously a mistake to class such a man with the realists or naturalists who place scientific before artistic considerations, though it is easy to understand how the Mid-Victorians made such a blunder. They confused what the language of the schools describes as objective idealism with subjective idealism. Compared with the emptiness and vapidity of a Barret, Cox may well have seemed realistic and naturalistic. But his work has nothing of the disjunctive observation or cold-blooded, rationalistic, inventory-making of a typical realist like John Brett. Cox paints what Reynolds has called "the unadulterated habits of nature." He never aims at "deceiving{19} the eye," "nor will he waste a moment upon those smaller objects which only serve to catch the sense" and "divide the attention." The one great design he always keeps in view is that of "speaking to the heart."

It would be useless to pretend that Cox is altogether free from the defects of his qualities. He is often too general, vague and empty. Sometimes he is passive and timid, as though he hoped to get his effects by merely "leaving out," or by overlooking and scorning the individuality of natural objects. But he possesses in abundance the great and inspiriting virtues of the idealists, as well as some of their defects. He takes us away from the world of bare unrelated fact into regions where the human consciousness can beat its wings and feel glad. His art is of the centre, thoroughly typical and national. He deals only with essentials, with those dumb longings and primary passions that form the obscure groundwork of life itself. His place is certainly among the great figures of English art, beside Constable and Cozens and Girtin, as one of the seers and prophets of the tenderness and strength of the nation's character.

I should like to take this opportunity to thank Mr. A. Walker, of 118, New Bond Street—to whose kindness the publishers and editor are indebted for permission to publish this selection from Cox's drawings and sketches—for his courtesy in permitting me to examine at my leisure the whole of the drawings, sketches and sketch books of David Cox which he is fortunate enough to possess.

PLATE II

OLD WESTMINSTER

PLATE III

PEASANTS ON HORSEBACK

PLATE IV

A ROADSIDE COTTAGE

PLATE V

NEAR DINAS MOWDDWY, MERIONETHSHIRE

PLATE VI

A FISHING VILLAGE

PLATE VII

NEAR KENILWORTH

PLATE VIII

CHEPSTOW

PLATE IX

SCENE IN NORTH WALES

PLATE X

A VILLAGE STREET

PLATE XI

FOREGROUND STUDY

PLATE XII

CHEPSTOW BRIDGE AND CASTLE

PLATE XIII

STUDY OF TREES

PLATE XIV

VIEW IN NORTH WALES

PLATE XV

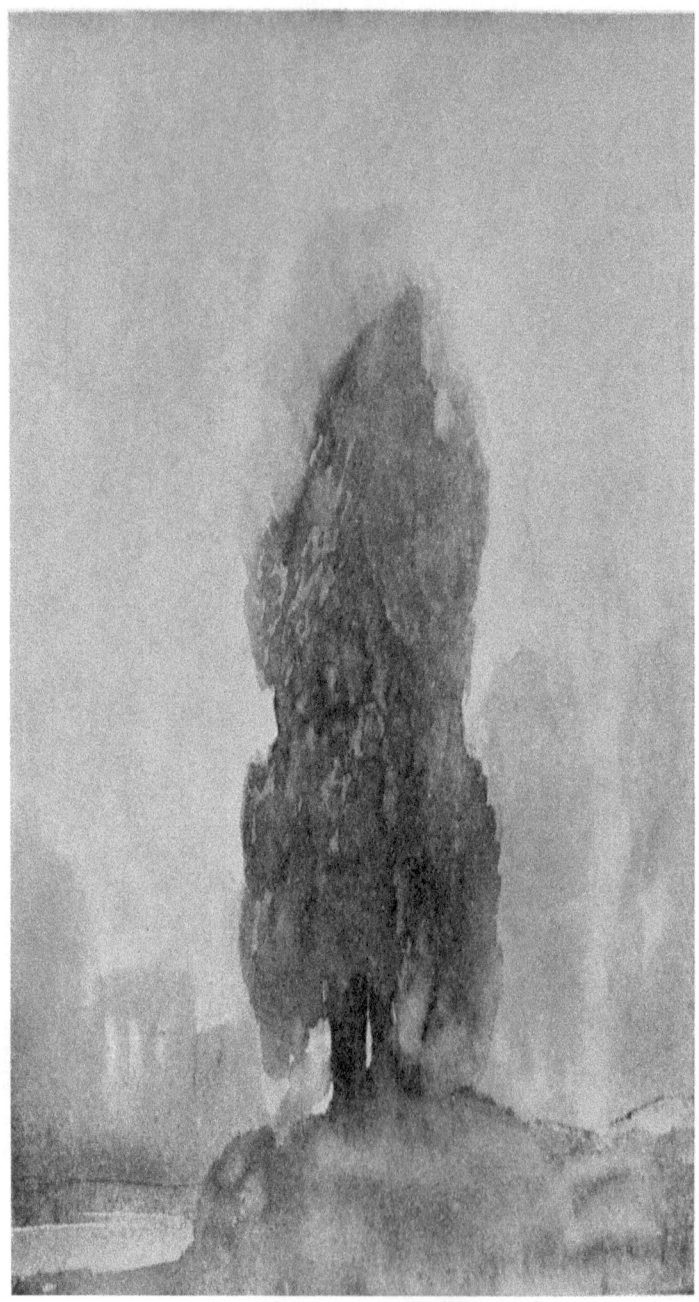

EARLY MORNING MIST

PLATE XVI

LLANRWST

PLATE XVII

HARDWICK

PLATE XVIII

NEAR BIRMINGHAM

PLATE XIX

AUTUMN WOODS

PLATE XX

KIRKBY STEPHEN

PLATE XXI

MOUNTAIN AND STREAM, NORTH WALES

PLATE XXII

ARCHITECTURAL STUDY

PLATE XXIII

GOODRICH CASTLE

PLATE XXIV

NEAR KENILWORTH CASTLE

PLATE XXV

THE SALT MARSH

PLATE XXVI

KNOLE HOUSE, KENT

PLATE XXVII

THE BEACH

PLATE XXVIII

WINDY WEATHER

PLATE XXIX

A STUDY OF TREES

PLATE XXX

CARNARVON CASTLE

PLATE XXXI

ON THE MOOR

PLATE XXXII

CLAPHAM, YORKSHIRE

PLATE XXXIII

THE HILL SIDE

PLATE XXXIV

LOW TIDE

PLATE XXXV

LLAUGHARNE CASTLE, CARMARTHEN BAY

PLATE XXXVI

SKETCH OF ROCKS AND CASTLE

PLATE XXXVII

DUTCH COAST SCENE

PLATE XXXVIII

SCENE IN NORTH WALES

PLATE XXXIX

NEAR RADLETT

PLATE XL

NEAR KENILWORTH

PLATE XLI

ROTTERDAM

PLATE XLII

TREFKIW, NEAR LLANRWST

PLATE XLIII

THE INN YARD

PLATE XLIV

OLD WESTMINSTER

CPSIA information can be obtained
at www.ICGtesting.com
Printed in the USA
BVHW071953011121
620451BV00002B/283